The Life Cycle of a

Chicken

by Lisa Trumbauer

Consulting Editor: Gail Saunders-Smith, Ph.D.

Consultant: Ronald L. Rutowski, Professor,
Department of Biology, Arizona State University

Pebble Books

an imprint of Capstone Press
Mankato, Minnesota

Pebble Books are published by Capstone Press
151 Good Counsel Drive, P.O. Box 669, Mankato, Minnesota 56002
http://www.capstone-press.com

1 2 3 4 5 6 07 06 05 04 03 02

Library of Congress Cataloging-in-Publication Data
Trumbauer, Lisa, 1963–
The life cycle of a chicken/by Lisa Trumbauer.
p. cm.—(Life cycles)
Includes bibliographical references (p. 23) and index.
Summary: Text and photographs present a brief description of the life cycle
of chickens.
ISBN 0-7368-1183-4
1. Chickens—Life cycles—Juvenile literature. [1. Chickens.] I. Title. II. Life cycles
(Mankato, MN.)
SF487.5 .T78 2002
636.5—dc21   2001003109

Note to Parents and Teachers

The Life Cycles series supports national science standards related to life science. This book describes and illustrates the life cycle of a leghorn chicken. The photographs support early readers in understanding the text. The repetition of words and phrases helps early readers learn new words. This book also introduces early readers to subject-specific vocabulary words, which are defined in the Words to Know section. Early readers may need assistance to read some words and to use the Table of Contents, Words to Know, Read More, Internet Sites, and Index/Word List sections of the book.

Table of Contents

Photographs in this book show the life cycle of a leghorn chicken.

egg

A chicken begins
life as an egg.

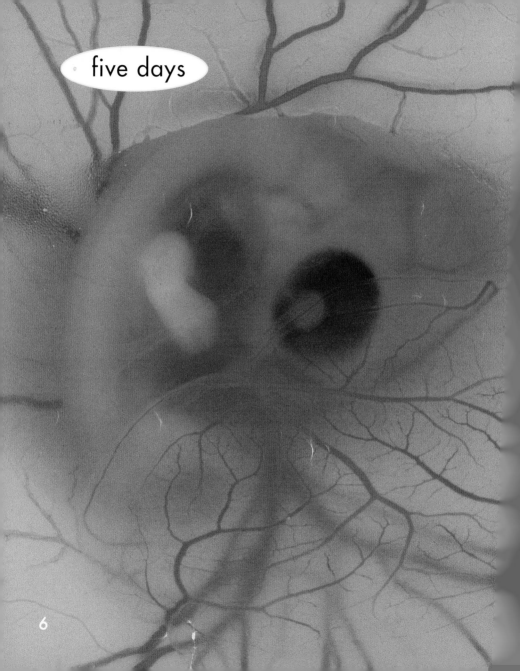

five days

A chick grows inside
the egg for 21 days.

21 days

The egg breaks
and the wet chick hatches.

chick

Yellow down covers
the chick's body.

six weeks

Long feathers grow
on the chick's body
after six weeks.

adult

The chick becomes
an adult. Chickens
can live up to 12 years.

A male chicken is
a rooster. He shows
his feathers and crows
to attract a hen. A hen
is a female chicken.
The two chickens mate.

Then the hen lays
one egg. She sits
on the egg to keep
it warm.

chick

egg

six weeks

adult

20

The egg is the start
of a new life cycle.

(Words to Know

attract—to get the attention of someone or something; when chickens are attracted to each other, they move closer to one another.

down—the soft feathers of a young chicken

egg—the first life stage of a chicken; growing chicks use the yolk inside the egg for food.

feather—one of the light, fluffy parts that cover a bird's body

hatch—to break out of an eggshell

hen—a female chicken who is able to mate; most hens lay one egg each day.

life cycle—the stages in the life of an animal; the life cycle includes being born, growing up, having young, and dying.

mate—to join together to produce young

rooster—a male chicken who is able to mate; roosters display or show their feathers to hens when they are ready to mate.

Read More

Powell, Jillian. *From Chick to Chicken.* How Do They Grow? Austin, Texas: Raintree Steck-Vaughn, 2001.

Schuh, Mari C. *Chickens on the Farm.* On the Farm. Mankato, Minn.: Pebble Books, 2002.

Stone, Lynn M. *Chickens Have Chicks.* Animals and Their Young. Minneapolis: Compass Point Books, 2000.

Internet Sites

Chicken Facts
http://www.ces.ncsu.edu/lenoir/staff/jnix/pubs/an.workbook/chickens.html

Chicken Printout
http://www.enchantedlearning.com/subjects/birds/printouts/chickenprintout.shtml

Chickens
http://www.kidsfarm.com/chickens.htm

Index/Word List

adult, 15
attract, 17
becomes, 15
begins, 5
body, 11, 13
breaks, 9
covers, 11
crows, 17
egg, 5, 7, 9, 19, 21
feathers, 13, 17
female, 17

grow, 7, 13
hatches, 9
hen, 17, 19
lays, 19
life cycle, 21
live, 15
male, 17
mate, 17
rooster, 17
warm, 19
wet, 9

Word Count: 103
Early-Intervention Level: 14

Editorial Credits

Sarah Lynn Schuette, editor; Jennifer Schonborn, production designer and interior illustrator; Kia Bielke, cover designer; Kimberly Danger and Mary Englar, photo researchers

Photo Credits

Dwight R. Kuhn, cover, 1, 4, 8, 10, 12, 14, 16, 18, 20 (all)
Visuals Unlimited/Jerome Wexler, 6